Librarians
Then and Now

Roben Alarcon, M.A.Ed.

Contributing Author
Jill K. Mulhall, M.Ed.

Associate Editor
Christina Hill, M.A.

Assistant Editor
Torrey Maloof

Editorial Director
Emily R. Smith, M.A.Ed.

Project Researcher
Gillian Eve Makepeace

Editor-in-Chief
Sharon Coan, M.S.Ed.

Editorial Manager
Gisela Lee, M.A.

Creative Director
Lee Aucoin

Illustration Manager
Timothy J. Bradley

Designers
Lesley Palmer
Debora Brown
Zac Calbert
Robin Erickson

Project Consultant
Corinne Burton, M.A.Ed.

Publisher
Rachelle Cracchiolo, M.S.Ed.

Teacher Created Materials

5301 Oceanus Drive
Huntington Beach, CA 92649-1030
http://www.tcmpub.com

ISBN 978-0-7439-9376-0

© *2007 Teacher Created Materials, Inc.*

Table of Contents

Fact Finder

Librarians help people check out books. They keep track of the books, too. But, that is not all they do. Librarians show people the best ways to use libraries. They know how to find what people need. They help others get **information**.

◀ This girl is checking out a library book.

Library ▶ check-out slip

▲ Benjamin Franklin helped open a library.

The First Libraries in America

Long ago, Benjamin Franklin had a good idea. He wanted to open a place where people could share books. So, he started a library. It was like a club. People had to pay money to join. Then, they became **members**. Each member read a lot of books. This helped them learn.

Only One Book?

The settlers that first came to the United States did not read much. They did not have time. They had too much work to do. Most families only had one book in their homes. That book was the Bible.

⬇ These cloth makers were too busy to read books.

Renting A Good Story

▲ Bookmobiles are libraries that travel to where people live. Long ago, they were in horse-drawn carts.

Soon, more people wanted to read. So, new libraries were opened. These libraries rented out books. A person could pay by the hour or by the day. The owners hoped to make a lot of money.

Most of these books were **fiction** (FIK-shuhn). They were fun and exciting stories. People were no longer reading just to learn. They found out that reading was fun, too!

The Denver Public Library ➡ bookmobile was a trailer.

↟ The Erie Canal

A Floating Library

For years, the "Book Boat" went up and down the Erie Canal. It would stop to let people rent books. The books cost 2 cents for each hour or ten cents for the whole day.

Reading for Free

Laws were passed that made it free for students to go to school. People thought libraries should be free, too. This is how public libraries came to be. They were paid for with tax money. So, anyone could check out a book!

Librarians were **hired** to be in charge. At that time, many librarians were also teachers.

♦ Children read in a library in 1910.

A Library with No Books

One of the very first public libraries was in Egypt (EE-jipt). It did not have books. It had **scrolls**.

This library ➡ from ancient Egypt was full of paper scrolls.

The Largest Library

The largest library in the world is the Library of Congress. It is in Washington, D.C. It has over 29 million books.

First the Men, Then the Women

The first librarians were men. Then, the pay for the job went down. Some men did not want the job anymore. They became library **directors**.

Today, the job has changed. Many librarians are now women. There are also female library directors. These women help run the library. They order the tools the library needs. They train other librarians, too.

Dewey's Decimals

Melvil Dewey loved math when he was a boy. At college, he worked as a librarian. He wanted to put the books in a better order. So, he decided to use numbers. He made the **Dewey Decimal System**. This system is now used around the world. Today, books in libraries are organized by using numbers.

Melvil Dewey

All Male Librarians

In Vatican City, all of the librarians are men. This is because they are all **priests**. The pope lives in Vatican City. This is the center of the Catholic Church. Vatican City is in the middle of Rome.

▲ This building is called Saint Peter's.
The Vatican library is the building on the right.

Learning to Be a Librarian

At first, librarians were called library keepers. They only had to take care of the books. They did not need a lot of education.

Today, librarians must do many different tasks. They need to learn special skills. To learn these skills, they must go to school. First, they get a college **degree**. Then, they have to get a special library degree.

⬇ This woman just got her degree to become a librarian.

Other Things to Learn

Most public libraries provide services. Some libraries have a children's story time. Others have classes to teach people how to read. Librarians are in charge of these programs.

⬥ Children gather around a librarian during story time.

▲ The books are very thick in law libraries.

Different Kinds of Librarians

Librarians can work for public libraries. They can also work for schools or colleges. School librarians need a teaching degree in some states.

Some libraries only have special kinds of books. Law libraries only carry law books. There are also libraries just for science books. Librarians who work in these libraries need to know a lot about these subjects.

Canada

United States

Teacher-Librarians

In Canada, school librarians are called teacher-librarians. This is because they must be teachers first.

This librarian helps a student find the book she needs.

New Ways to Learn

The first libraries only had books. That is what librarians used for information. Each book title was listed on a card. These cards were kept in a big cabinet called a **card catalog**.

Today, libraries have much more than books. They carry newspapers, magazines, movies, and music. Librarians organize all these different **resources** (REE-sohr-ses). They make them easy to use.

⬇ This girl uses a computer to find a book.

Choosing New Books

Librarians help choose which new books to buy for their libraries. Most libraries do not have much money. So, they try to buy the books that the people in their communities need the most.

People used card catalogs to find books. Now, they use computers.

▲ A librarian helps a man find information.

▲ Students using computers in a library

Technology Teachers

Teaching has always been part of a librarian's job. Librarians show people how to find books. They teach people how to read, too.

Now, librarians also teach people how to use **technology**. Most libraries have computers and the **Internet**. Some libraries use **CD-ROMs**. Librarians teach people how to use these new tools.

The large yellow machine is a robot. It pulls down boxes from the high shelves.

Robots in the Library

There is a huge library in Las Vegas, Nevada. It cost $51 million to build. There are special robots that pull books down from the high shelves.

After the robot gets a box, a librarian can pull out the book she wants.

Growing and Changing

Librarians still take care of books. But, their duties have grown. Today, libraries are very big. Many librarians work in just one part of the library. They learn as much as they can about special subjects. Some librarians teach classes. Others are there to help children.

▲ Libraries today have lots of books for us to read.

Even though things have changed, librarians still have the same goal. They help us learn. They make sure that we know how to find the books we want. And, they show us that reading is fun!

⬆ This librarian helps a child learn how to read.

A Day in the Life Then

Arna Bontemps (1902–1973)

Arna Bontemps (bahn-TAHM) was a writer. He wrote lots of poetry. He also wrote books for children. And, he loved to read. So, he went to college. There, he learned how to be a librarian. He got a job as a school librarian. He helped add a new part of the library. It had books on African Americans.

Let's pretend to ask Arna Bontemps some questions about his job.

Why did you decide to be a librarian?

I was confused when I was in school. There were very few books on African

Americans. I couldn't read about people like me. So, I fixed this problem. I ordered different kinds of books. Now, students can learn about many kinds of people.

What is your day like?

I do a lot of research. I help students find books. They are happy when I find the right books for them. I know where to find all the books in our library. I also study a lot. And, of course, I read!

What do you like most about your job?

I learn new things each day. I meet a lot of students. They also love to read. Libraries are special places. They are tools for learning!

◆ This is Fisk University. This is where Mr. Bontemps was head librarian.

Tools of the Trade Then

◀ These librarians used a card catalog. People searched the card catalog for the books they wanted. The cards told them where to find the books.

Librarians used to stamp ▶ checkout cards. This was how they kept track of books. Many libraries today use computers to do this.

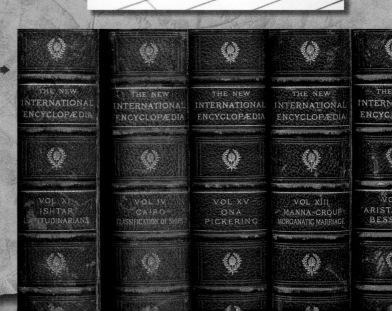

Encyclopedias ▶ have a lot of information in them. Librarians use them to help people learn. Today, many encyclopedias are online.

Tools of the Trade Now

Librarians use stools ➤ to reach books that are on high shelves.

Children's
X372 – X399

Nonfiction
X400 – X591.6

⬆ Today, most libraries use the Dewey Decimal System. It is a great tool for sorting books.

◄ Today, many libraries have computers. Their card catalogs can be found online. And, encyclopedias are now online. This makes it easier and faster to find information.

A Day in the Life Now

Orion Tippens

Orion Tippens is a library assistant at his local library in the city of Lake Forest. He has been working at the library for three years. In his free time he likes to write. He is also a college student.

Why did you decide to become a librarian?

I had a friend who worked at the library. He told me about the job. So, I thought I would apply. It was a good decision. I like my job. I think that a librarian's job is an important one.

What is your day like?

I like being able to serve the public. I get to talk to new people every day. Also, I help people find books. And, I learn something new every day!

What do you like most about your job?

The best thing about my job is the people I meet. I like being a part of my community. Every day I get to meet other community members. I really like this part of my job.

⬇ Mr. Tippens works in a library just like this one.

PUBLIC LIBRARY

BOOK DROP

Glossary

card catalog—a cabinet full of cards with book titles on them

CD-ROMs—CDs with information that can be seen on a computer

degree—a title people get when they finish college

Dewey Decimal System—a system that orders books using numbers and decimals

directors—people in charge of others

encyclopedias—books full of facts and information

fiction—made-up stories; not true stories or facts

hired—given a job

information—facts or things to know

Internet—computers connected around the world

members—people that are part of a group or club

priests—people who lead religious service

resources—things that can be used to help you

scrolls—rolls of paper with writing on them

technology—a new way of solving problems using tools or science

Index

Credits

Acknowledgements

Special thanks to Orion Tippens for providing the *Day in the Life Now* interview. Mr. Tippens is a library assistant in Lake Forest, California.

Image Credits

cover Eyewire; p.1 Eyewire; p.4 Photodisc; pp.4–5 iStockphoto.com/Stefan Klein; p.5 iStockphoto.com/Alexei Nabarro; p.6 The Granger Collection, New York; p.7 (top) iStockphoto.com/Gisele Wright; p.7 (bottom) The Granger Collection, New York; p.8 The Granger Collection, New York; p.9 (top) The Granger Collection, New York; p.9 (bottom) Denver Public Library; p.10 The Library of Congress; p.11 (top) The Granger Collection, New York; p.11 (middle) Clipart. com; p.11 (bottom) Jason Maehl/Shutterstock, Inc.; p.12 Dover Publications; p.13 Joyce Sherwin/Shutterstock, Inc.; p.14 Photodisc; p.15 (top) Teacher Created Materials; p.15 (bottom) Denver Public Library; p.16 The Library of Congress; p.17 (top) Lesley/Digital Wisdom; p.17 (bottom) Photodisc; p.18 Gudelia Marmion/Shutterstock, Inc.; p.19 Stephen Coburn/Shutterstock, Inc.; p.20 (left) Photos.com; p.20 (middle) Photos.com; p.20 (right) Photodisc; p.21 (top) Courtesy of the Lied Library, Las Vegas/Aaron Mayes; p.21 (bottom) Courtesy of the Lied Library, Las Vegas/Aaron Mayes; p.22 Photos.com; p.23 Marmion/ Shutterstock, Inc.; p.24 The Library of Congress; p.25 The Library of Congress; p.26 (top) The Library of Congress; p.26 (middle) Scott Rothstein/Shutterstock, Inc.; p.26 (bottom)Weldon Schloneger/Shutterstock, Inc.; p.27 (top) Courtesy of Christina Hill; p.27 (middle) Courtesy of Christina Hill; p.27 (bottom) iStockphoto.com/ImagesbyTrista; p.28 Courtesy of Orion Tippens; p.29 Lisa C. McDonald/Shutterstock, Inc.; back cover The Library of Congress